THOUGHTS FOR THE

THOUGHTFUL

BY

HENRY CLAY MORRISON

First Fruits Press
Wilmore, Kentucky
c2013

ISBN: 9781621711377 (Print), 9781621711384 (Digital)

Thoughts for the Thoughtful by Henry Clay Morrison
First Fruits Press, © 2013
Previously published by the Pentecostal Publishing Company, 1912

Digital version at
http://place.asburyseminary.edu/firstfruitsheritagematerial/69/

For all other uses, contact:

First Fruits Press
B.L. Fisher Library
Asbury Theological Seminary
204 N. Lexington Ave.
Wilmore, KY 40390
http://place.asburyseminary.edu/firstfruits

Morrison, H. C. (Henry Clay), 1857-1942.
Thoughts for the thoughtful / by Henry Clay Morrison.
    56 p. ; 21 cm.
    Wilmore, Ky. : First Fruits Press, c2013.
    Reprint. Previously published: Louisville, Ky. : Pentecostal Pub. Co., 1912.
    ISBN: 9781621711377 (pbk.)
    1. Christian life -- Methodist authors. I. Title.
    BV4510 .M68 2013   242

Cover design by Haley Hill

asburyseminary.edu
800.2ASBURY
204 North Lexington Avenue
Wilmore, Kentucky 40390

First Fruits
THE ACADEMIC OPEN PRESS OF ASBURY SEMINARY

Thoughts
For The
Thoughtful

BY

REV. H. C. MORRISON

Editor the Pentecostal Herald.
Author, World Tour of Evangelism, Life Sketches and Sermons,
The Two Lawyers, Baptism with the Holy Ghost, Sec-
ond Coming, Pearl of Greatest Price.

PENTECOSTAL PUBLISHING COMPANY
LOUISVILLE, KY.

CHAPTER I.

That church organization most scriptural in doctrine, with the deepest spirituality in life, most practical and consistent in the service of God and humanity, with the broadest democracy in government, is the church most pleasing to God, and most desirable to men of true piety and strong intelligence.

The church that would abide and bless the race must be apostolic in teaching, in organization, in the inner motives that control its leaders, in the wide scope of its operation, and the great end toward which it works—The exaltation of Jesus Christ and the salvation of a lost race.

The Church of Christ is no place for the spirit of the autocrat or tyrant, but the spirit of brotherly love, the spirit that prefers one above the other, where the winning of souls and the building up and per-

fecting of the saints is the great impell-
ing motive that rules the hearts of those
members who guide and lead in the
church.

In His teachings, Jesus was
careful to caution us against any sort
of pride or ambition for place and
power among our brethren in the
church, but we were to cultivate the
spirit that serves. In humility and love,
we were to wash each other's feet.

The spirit of autocracy in the Church
of Christ destroys the spirit of true
brotherhood, of genuine religion; it
makes men self-seeking, it fosters the
spirit of rulership, it develops tyranny,
it quenches life and liberty, it interferes
with growth, it dwarfs the mind and
darkens the soul.

If we would grow great men
in brain and heart, we must give
them large liberty; they must have
room for expansion, freedom of mind
for flight in the open sunlight of truth

and progress. They must think, speak, and act without any cringing fear of some human master.

Ironclad ecclesiasticisms, human dictators, and ambitious rulers in the church who put up one and put down another, in order to foster and advance their own selfish ends or whims would greatly hinder the progress of the kingdom of God in the world.

If a man must stifle his best thoughts, and murder within himself the desire for high and noble action because of the prejudices and interference of some ecclesiastical dictator, he must of necessity be a dwarfed man, a mere human machine, and in the end a dangerous tool in the hands of the tyrant.

Some months ago I saw an immigrant, evidently from southern Europe, who had just landed on our shores. He had a small, weak-looking body, a little ill-

shaped head, and a pinched, blank
face. Ignorance, timidity, and fear
characterized his every look and movement. He was the logical outcome of
centuries of subjugation to the whims
and caprices of popes and kings. He
had been cast in a small mold and
forced into a narrow groove. He had
submitted to a tyranny that had crushed
him until there was hardly any soul left
in him. He was most all animal and a
very poor specimen of animal.

A big American passed by at the
same time with his head up, and his
shoulders back, and his face shining
with intelligence. There was freedom
in his every movement; he was a good
member of society; he had helped to
make that society. He was under law,
but he had a voice and a vote in fram-
ing the law. He respected the magis-
trates, but he had helped to elect them,
and they were public servants to be dis-
charged if they failed to perform their
duties, or infringe upon the rights of the
people.

He was a member of the church, but he called no man master; he was one of a band of brethren standing on an equal footing with all the rest. They elected their officials who were in no sense their dictators. He followed, with his brethren, their spiritual, God-given leaders in pressing the work of salvation, but carried with him always a sense of religious liberty, of freedom of mind and soul. He lived in the midst of surroundings and breathed an atmosphere that makes men large, free and brave; strong of soul noble in heart, and lofty in character It had cost much struggle, and battle, and tears, and bloodshed to make such a man a possibility, but the product was well worth all it cost.

We are in great danger that in our church affairs we become ironclad in government and the control and direction of the affairs of the kingdom. In a word, that we become governmental and formal, rather than evangelical and spiritual. It is possible that we may create offices and put men into them with large salaries and great power over their brethren, who, in the end, will become ecclesiastical rulers instead of spiritual guides, and examples of piety and devoted zeal to their Master.

It would be unfortunate indeed if the church should create places carrying with them so much financial renumeration, so much honor among men, and so much authority over men, that she produce in her ministry an itching for office, drawing the souls of her sons away from the one great work of winning souls to Christ, to become mere office-seekers, hungering and thirsting after place; a group from this section of the church trading with a group from some other part, and secretly forming combinations to sell so many votes for your man, in order that you turn over so many votes for our man for secretary or agent, or editor or other high place; meanwhile keeping an innocent look on the surface as if nothing was going on, so as to decieve others and land one's candidate into the desired place without arousing opposition.

Such a thing would grieve the Holy Ghost. It would hinder the progress of that holiness which God raised up the church to spread over the earth; in the end it would permeate the church with a spirit of unrest and dissatisfaction, and in time it would put into office and leadership a class of men who care but little for the spiritual welfare of the people, for the peace and holiness of the flock, but who long for power and who would elevate those who rallied to their standard, and put to disadvantage those who opposed their ambitious purposes.

When such men achieve their purpose, when they get into power, when they rule and reign and direct and control the affairs of the earthly kingdom, you may bid farewell to church discipline.

They are not going to object to

the people dancing, playing cards, attending theaters, and indulging in other forms of worldliness, provided the people rally to their standards and keep them in power. And you may be sure that the worldly-loving people will seek to keep such men in power, and under such circumstances you may bid farewell to the great doctrine of depravity, the natural sinfulness of the heart. Such a doctrine is repulsive to such leaders and such followers. It is too humiliating for their contemplation and approval.

You may bid farewell to profound conviction for sin, a great struggle of pentitent souls at altars of prayer and clear regeneration by the power of the Spirit; you may bid farewell to the doctrine of entire sanctification; it calls for too high a surrender of all that is worldly, it asks for too deep a consecration, it sets up too high a standard of holiness, it goes too deep into the supernatural. In the nature of things, it sweeps away all the spirit of office seeking and of dictatorial rulership and exaltation of mere men, human ambitions, and human authority which has no warrant in the word of God.

Such a condition of things in the Church of Christ would be calamitous indeed, and yet such a condition is a possibility. There seems to be in human nature a strong natural drift in this direction. Men love place and honor and power among their brethren. It is easy for a man to drift from the high currents of evangelism to the lower currents of ecclesiasticism. It is easy for human nature to find itself longing for power over man, rather than for power with God, and is it not time that we looked about us and guard against the dangerous drift toward these unfortunate conditions? Ought not the church seek to prevent the spirit of office seeking by making fewer offices and making them less attractive: Less power for instance, smaller salaries, while she exalts more

and more the preaching of the word of
God, the promotion of revivals of religion, the winning of the souls of men
from sin to Christ.

Let the entire church exalt the
preacher above the official. The highest
place that mortal man can occupy is
that of the untrammeled messenger of
the Lord. Strip officialism of some of
its chief attractions, and teach the people the greatest work in the church is
the preaching of the word and the
rescuing of the lost. Might it not be
a good idea, in so far as it is possible,
to put consecrated, wide-awake laymen
into office for the management of the
material things of the church? That
would be apostolic. The disciples
selected Stephen and others to look
after material things, in order that they
might give themselves to fasting, to
prayer, and to the preaching of the
word. If God calls a man to preach,
why should he come down from his
high place to serve in mere business
matters? Why should he descend from

the pulpit to any office however great or lucrative? *Why should there be any great offices in the Church of God?* Let men who are called to preach, preach the word; let their hearts yearn and break with sorrow and longing for souls. Make it a point to get all of your church offices down somewhere in the neighborhood of the teachings of Jesus Christ.

There are plenty of gifted men who can fill any modest office in the church which is in harmony and keeping with New Testament Christianity. There are many men creating a stir in the world, pressing the battle for the salvation of souls and contributing no little to the uplift of their fellow beings, who have never had an office, who have never desired place or power among their brethren in the kingdom of Christ.

Saint Paul was never in office, he never was a candidate, but he was a chosen vessel of the Lord, and a great preacher of truth. John the Beloved, Martin Luther, John Wesley, Charles Spurgeon, Charles Finney, Dwight Moody and a great host of shining souls who have been the salt of the earth and the light of the world, never were in high office in the Church of God. They were ministers of the gospel of Jesus and that is one of the highest positions that any man can occupy.

Let us exalt the preaching of the gospel and the winning of souls and be done with noise, desire and strifes for office, the increase of offices, the increase of salaries for those in office, and the increase of power for those in office. We are in danger that we shall burden Christainity down with those things that did not exist in the Apostolic Church, and have no warrant in the word of God.

We must not burden ourselves and cut off our circulation and spirit of freedom with too much ecclesiastical harness. We must live and labor on a scriptural basis; we must have the leadership of the Holy Ghost; each individual man must be conscious of his presence. We must stand on one broad platform of brotherhood and equality in the Church of God.

CHAPTER II.

A SERIOUS AND DELICATE SITUATION.

One of the most serious and delicate problems confronting the American people, is the rapid increase and aggressiveness of Roman Catholicism in the United States.

A very large per cent of the immigrants coming from Europe are Roman Catholics and, it may be truthfully said that a very large per cent of these immigrants are people of a very low grade of intelligence and piety and are poorly prepared for citizenship.

The Methodist Church, taking in the whole family of Methodist organizations in this country, boasts of something like five million members. With the present rate of immigration, that many foreigners will come to our shores in four years and perhaps three-fourths of them will be Roman Catholics.

If immigrants to this country are as numerous for the next decade as they have been for the past five years, we may safely count on five million of Catholics landing on these shores within the next seven years, and, while we would not misrepresent these people, it is safe to say that they know almost nothing of the Bible; they are very illiterate, they have but little conception of the sacred- ness of the Sabbath, they can contri- bute almost nothing to the intellectual, moral, and spiritual life of the nation.

The Catholic Church in this country is becoming remarkably aggressive. That the hearts of the Pope, cardinals and bishops are set on the United States, there is no doubt. Why should it not be so? The Catholics certainly be- lieve themselves to be right and that the propagation of their doctrines is for the welfare of the race.

There is no part of the world today that offers so rich a har- vest field for evangelism and propa⁻

gandism as this country. Here we have
the mixed multitudes from all nations,
of all colors, speaking all languages.
Here we have the most splendid enter-
prises for the advancement of agricul-
ture, manufacture and commerce. Here
we have the largest accumulations of
capital in the world and the best pos
sibilities for individual successes to be
found anywhere. Why should not
Romanism set its heart for the con-
quest of the United States?

The Pope is constantly sending over
greetings and blessings. His envoys
are frequently visiting this country and
are received with great honor and mag-
nificent parade in our largest cities.
Cathedrals, costing into the millions of
dollars, have been and are being erect-
ed in our great centers of population,
which give wonderful prestige and
power to Romanism among the people.
Great pageants with marching columns,
bands of music, and banners are to be
seen on many occasions in American
cities, with distinguished Romanists rid-

ing in carriages, arousing the zeal of their own people, and making a profound impression upon the common masses who are outside of any church. All of these things are having a powerful influence for Rome.

The problem of meeting the situation is difficult for many reasons. You may be sure that statesmen—politicians rather, are going to be very shrewd and careful in making any reference derogatory to Romanism. The Catholic vote is a powerful influence in politics in this country and no politician is willing to array this vote against himself.

The same is true of the secular press. The great newspapers of the country would not dare to make any sort of aggressive opposition against Romanism. Such a move would, at once, bring them financial loss. Catholic people would boycott any paper that devoted its columns to pointing out the dangers which threaten our country from the Romish Church. I am not blaming the Catholics for this, it is perfectly natural that they should do so, and we all know they would do so. What church would be willing to support politicians or papers who would in turn attack that church and its interests and methods of propaganda?

It is equally true of men in the commercial world. Business men will be very careful in giving expression of disapproval of anything leading Catholics may say or undertake in their purpose to advance the interest of their church in this country. Such men would at once suffer in their trade. The whole Catholic fraternity stands together and would certainly not patronize men who opposed the growth and denomination of their church and its institutions.

The reader may ask, why do we object to the growth of Catholicism? To which we answer, first of all: The Bible, the public school and the Protestant Church are the great factors which have made our American civilization possible. They have been the chief corner-stones of our liberties. The Bible has revealed to us the will of God and the just and equal laws with which He proposes to regulate and elevate the race.

The schools have educated and developed our intellectual life. The Protestant Church has disseminated the Scriptures, proclaimed the gospel, appealed to our consciences, warned us of the dangers of sin, held up before us the crucified Christ, and called the lost multitudes to trust, not in forms, or popes, or priests, but in the Christ of Calvary, for the forgiveness of sins.

The Romish Church arrays herself with all her power, against the Bible, the public schools, and Protestantism. It would take the Bible out of the hands of the people; it would close the public schools against our millions of happy children; it would shut the doors of every Protestant Church in our great republic. It would blot out the sacred fires that burn on a million family altars throughout the nation.

With her views of God and His revelation, the Pope, and the means and methods of salvation, she is bound by conscience, to disapprove of, and desire the destruction of, these three greatest means of grace and progress in America. She has boldly objected to the use of the Scriptures in our public schools. If it were in her power, she would take the Bible off of our family altars, and leave us without the word to guide us, and put us at the feet of priests with burning tapers, to learn our lessons of truth and piety.

The Catholic Church has a history. A history of blood and fire and persecution. The Catholic Church has not changed. Her narrowness and prejudice are the same that they have been through the centuries. She believes absolutely in herself. Her bigotry has been revealed time and again in a remarkable way in the past few months.

In Spain she drove a member of the royal family from office because he married a Protestant woman.

The Pope at Rome refused to meet a prominent American citizen because he attended a Methodist Church. He could not give audience to an ex-President of this nation because that ex-President would not pledge himself that, while in Rome, he would not attend a Protestant Church. Could anything be more narrow? Can the reader conceive of bigotry more rank? Give men great ecclesiastical and political power, with views like these, and think of what the result would be. How soon our religious liberties would vanish, and the progress of the intellectual and spiritual life of the nation be stopped and reversed.

Catholicism has had ample opportunity for the development of great peoples. How signally she has failed, Italy, France, Spain, bear sad witness,

No church could wish a better opportunity for evangelism of any peoples than Catholocism has had in Cuba, Porto Rico, and the Philippine Islands, and behold the intellectual and moral degradation of those peoples. Wherever the shadow of St. Peter falls, men are dwarfed in mind and spirit and body.

The whole spirit of Romanism is contrary to the entire spirit of democracy, and the institutions of freedom which democracy propagates and nurtures. It is not strange that Catholic conventions were passing resolutions disapproving of the overthrow of the throne in Portugal and the setting up of a republican form of government. The spirit of freedom is contrary to the spirit of Romanism.

When men become properly educated, when men get correct conceptions of God, of themselves and their relations to the divine government and human society, they

are unfit for good Romanists. Ignorance, superstition, the spirit of submis-
siveness to tyranny, obedience to men,
the worshiping of images, the stupidity
which will spend large sums of money
for prayers and masses for the dead—
these things go into the making up of a
condition of society in which Romanism flourishes.

CHAPTER III.

THE SACREDNESS AND OPPORTUNITIES OF MOTHERHOOD.

In the midst of the confusion and strife with reference to the suffragette, woman's rights, and other questions and debates arising with reference to woman's place in home and church and state, let us not forget motherhood and its sacred offices and opportunities.

Within the next few decades there are some fifteen hundred million of babies due to be born, nurtured, cared for, loved and labored with, and brought from helpless infancy to young man and womanhood. Think of the suffering, sorrow, the tears and agony and death involved in bringing into being, and up to the point of self-protection of this great army of human beings. If motherhood should fail, all things will fail.

If babies are not born, the
baby buggy factories will have to
make an assignment, the men
who make the little high chairs will go
out of business, the little wagon man
will have to seek other employment. the
toy man will have to find some other
job, it would become difficult to find
soldiers to fill up the depleted ranks of
armies, or hands to work factories, or
traveling men to sell goods, or business
men to buy them . If motherhood
should fail, then we will have to shut up
shop in a short time and close out all
business at the old stand and leave a
desolated world to moles and bats and
beasts.

After all, more depends upon motherhood than many of us had dreamed.
What could be more sacred than the
bringing into life teeming multitudes of
immortals in their beauty and strength
and power; what more honorable than
to nurse the nations at her breast, and
guide the young feet in their first totter-
ing steps and teach the little hands

their cunning, and the rosy lips to utter their first words and prayers. There can be no human office higher than that of motherhood, no human employment nobler than that of casting young life into the mold of rectitude and righteousness, than that of training the young for high thinking and noble action.

But because woman is to become a mother, and a mother is to become the moulder of the life and character that is to fashion the destiny of the nations for weal or woe, are we to conclude that mothers are fit for nothing more than to bear children and toil for them? Are the mothers of the land not most deeply interested in the welfare of the race in all its relationships in life? Is she not deeply concerned for the enactment of righteous laws, for good government, for the preservation of peace, for the education and uplifting of the children she hath borne?

Do not the mothers of the land constitute a very large per cent of the church membership, and shall they have nothing to say with reference to who shall stand in the pulpit, how the laws of the church shall be made, by whom administered, and how the affairs of the visible kingdom shall be directed in its human institutions and means of propagating the gospel? Does she not give and pray, and shall she not have her humble say in matters that have so much to do with those to whom she has given life and tending?

Shall mother have no word with reference to civic life? Shall she not have a choice with reference to those who make the laws and administer them? Does she not pay her taxes and give her sons to fight our battles? Shall she have no voice in whether there shall be peace or war and who shall direct the affairs that mean our weal or woe? Because she hath borne and nurtured us, toiled for us night and day, wept over us in our sins, and loved us through to light and hope; because she hath done these things so well shall we therefore say, there is nothing else that she can do?

After all, when we come to think, man boasts that it is his high privilege to care for and protect the women of the land. He claims that he would shield her from the ruder phases of life, that he will make laws and administer them for her protection and happiness. Has he done so well, has he protected her? Has he not turned the whiskey demon loose upon her home like a wild beast to rend her little one and leave her desolate? Has he not so guided the affairs of life that the trusts control the world's supplies, and laboring poverty goes in hunger and shivering rags? Is there not cruel neglect and unjust laws and graft and crime on every hand? Man boasts that he is woman's protector, that she must keep quiet while he fights her battles at the polls and in the legislative halls, but has he made his boast good?

We have a case in mind, a corporation not far from where we are writing.

The question up is wet or dry? Shall there be saloons, or shall there be none? Three-fourths of the property represented in this corporation is owned by people who stand for sobriety and order, but there is a large population of negroes, many of them idle and worse, but they have the power of suffrage; they can vote. They can trample down the rights of the people who pay the taxes, who support the church, who build the schools, who make the country blessed, who preserve the peace somewhat, and yet these illiterate black men who can be bought with a pint of adulterated whiskey, can go to the polls and vote the saloon into the town, and the mothers, the strong, true souls who bore us, who love us and who lead us to our Lord, must stand back in silence and see these poor ignorant creatures set and bait the traps to catch their sons. Do you tell me this is right? Will you try to make me believe that I must hush without protest and look in silence upon such ignorant, stupid cruelty?

It would seem that there is room for improvement in social and civic conditions, and that men should hush their boasts; we have failed so signally, woman has helped us in the midst of our failures so splendidly, can we not risk her in the councils of the church? Shall she not have a word to say with regard to who preaches to her and her children, and how laws are to be made and how administered and shall she have no choice in education, and in war, and temperance, in all the con⁻ flicts that go on about her here?

These are things of which we well may think, and in the midst of all, let us not forget that some fifteen hundred millions of babes are soon due to be born. The population now on the earth will soon be gone, their places must be taken by those who follow on to take up the load of life and carry it through the strife to their short end, and lay it down for other hands.

The reader understands that these thoughts are not so much to settle questions, but to raise them. To put the mind to work, to inquire into things, to ponder, to work out the solution of some of the problems of life. And, as the mind inquires, it will be asking if strife, in the political battle, on the hustings, and in the halls of legislation will be elevating to womanhood. Will she retain her modesty, her sensitiveness to evil, her high ideals? Will she continue to be the salt of the home, to sanctify and elevate the family circle, or will she become ambitious, coarse and selfish; and thus the mind will propose the questions which will arise.

If the home should fail, the state *Must* fail. If the fountain is impure, the stream must be impure. If womanhood should depart from God, from the holy altars of His church, from the love of tender babes wound in her fond embrace upon her breast, if she should prove untrue to her nature and to her high calling in the world, then all is lost. Our lines are broken everywhere, our defences are shattered, the advance of civilization is checked, the hosts of our hope are defeated, and the human race is put to rout .

While thinking let us not be discouraged. It is written in the Book, "The seed of the woman shall bruise the serpent's head." We may rest assured that at the close of the long conflict, there will come victory, there will be redemption at the last. The white banner of perfect peace will float in triumph over every battle field. Of course, no mere human agencies will bring this triumph in. The omnipotent arm of Jesus Christ alone can break the power of evil, and drive back the enemy. But when the victory is won, and the rewards for valiant services are given and the crowns are bestowed, mother sister, sweetheart, wife, and daughter shall have their part. How tenderly they have loved, how faithfully they have prayed, how patiently they have watched and waited through the weary

years, how gladly will they shout when
all the war is ended, and peace reigns
throughout the universe.

CHAPTER IV.

IF CHRIST SHOULD COME TO JERUSALEM?

It is suggestive of an interesting line of thought to ask one's self, "If Christ should come to Jerusalem and set up the kingdom of heaven on earth?"

The question naturally arises, what existing institutions in our civil, social and religious life would he overthrow and what would he perpetuate?

It is not unthinkable that Christ should come back to this earth. He came once to this globe, lived, labored and suffered here, why should he not come again?

All revelation with regard to Christ, indicates that he is deeply interested in the welfare and happiness of the human race. The whole story of his mission and work in the world, is a revelation of his love for mankind.

If he should come again, he would not come as a helpless babe in Bethlehem, to be hunted by jealous murderers, to grow up in seclusion, unheeded and unknown, to meet the opposition of stupid ignorance and prejudice.

He would not come back to be rejected by the church and to stand condemned before human tribunals, to be led to execution among criminals, to hang on the cross amidst the derision and ridicule of sinful men.

All of those tragic chapters in the history of Christ have passed forever. Their importance was incalculable, their significance was as deep as the depravity of the race, and high as the wants of immortal man, but all of that part of Christ's work *is finished.*

If he should come back to earth, it would be with such glory and power, that all the world that has read or heard the gospel story, would readily recognize him and submit to his will and supreme rulership. All kings and rulers would lay their crowns and scepters at his feet and bow in subjection to his dictatorship, or they would flee in fear and consternation from his glorious appearing.

Jesus Christ has come to have powerful influence in the world. The sinlessness of his character, the faultlessness of his conduct, the sublimity of his teaching, the unselfishness of his love and the patient forgiveness with which he suffered, have made him the *first* and *highest* of all beings who ever lived and walked in human form upon the earth.

Even those who deny the inspiration of the Scriptures, take off their hats to the faultless Man of Galilee. Those who claim that he was only a man, claim that he was by far the highest type of man that ever lived among men. Those who have believed in his deity, and yet have rejected his gospel, would fight to the death for the sake of the truths he taught and the church he has set up in the world.

Christ's life and teachings have, in a most wonderful way, affected architecture,, art and literature. His Spirit has permeated, to some extent, all civil government, social and commercial life. Jesus is the most familiar name in history; his sayings are repeated in courts, senates, congresses, cabinets, and about the camp-fires of the armies of the world. His life, and the precepts which fell from his lips, are thrilling the race with a new conception of duty and happiness and lifting the multitudes to a higher life.

If Jesus should come back to the earth in such a manner that there was no question as to his identity, so that all men could know, without doubt, that he was the Christ of Bethlehem, Nazareth, Gethsemane and the cross, the whole intelligent world would be thrilled and startled as by no other event that has occurred or could occur in all human history. As suggested at the outset, it is interesting to ask one's self, What institutions in our civil, social and religious life, would he overthrow and what would he perpetuate?

If Christ should return to reign on the earth it would seem that Jerusalem would be the most suitable and appropriate place for his headquarters. Above all other cities in the world, it is in human thought the most sacred. It is the religious center of the world's geography. Jews, Christians and Mohammedans alike, cherish for Jerusalem a reverence and love unknown for any other spot on earth. Abraham offered Isaac there, the ancient Jewish kings reigned there and made it famous throughout the inhabited world. Christ taught, suffered and died there. It was from Mt. Olivet, in full view of Jerusalem, that he ascended to heaven.

The Mohammedans associate Jerusalem with the most sacred things connected with their devotions. The loca-

tion would be about equally conven-
ient for the eastern and western world.
The Suez Canal opens up a highway
from all the East to Jerusalem. It
would be a splendid triumph for truth
and righteousness, if Christ, who rode
into Jerusalem on an asses' colt, to suffer upon a cross for a lost race, should
ride into Jerusalem upon the Shekinah
cloud and sit upon a throne of univer-
sal power to govern a redeemed race.

When we begin to think of the evils
in the world that Christ would overthrow, if he should return to reign on
earth, the whiskey traffic rises first in
our minds. Undoubtedly he would
sweep it out of existence. It is the
cause of more crime and disease, gaunt
poverty and human suffering, than any
other, and some people believe, than
all other evils in the world. Think
what a change the destruction of the
whiskey traffic would bring to the
world. If the millions of money
wasted in drink every year, was invest-
ed in comfortable homes, food and

clothing, it would go a long way toward relieving the world of its present state of suffering.

Put into bread, the grain that goes into intoxicants, and think of the mouths it would feed. How much sickness would disappear, how many prisons would stand empty, how many desolate homes would become happy, how many idle hands would seek useful and remunerative employment, how the earth would ring with songs of praise and shouts of joy, if Christ should come and sweep away the whiskey traffic. Our postmillennial friends who put off the coming of the Lord, may be sure that in this teaching, they have the most hearty approval and endorsement of the great host of Christless men engaged in the whiskey traffic, for they fully realize that his coming would prove disastrous to them and their business.

If Christ should come back to earth to reign, he would disband all of the

armies of the world. There would be
no more war, no need for soldiers; under his reign of love men would cease
to kill each other. There would be
millions of happy home-comings and
glad reunions; the military bands
would all come playing, "All hail the
power of Jesus' name"; the warships
of every nation would steam homeward
with the marine bands playing "Marching to Zion" and "Home Sweet
Home."

The vast amount of steel in
rifles, cannon, warships and fortifica-
tions, would be thrown into furnaces
and melted into ore and manufactured
into useful materials for building
homes, railways and ships for travel
and commerce. The men who have
wasted their lives in army camps, would
go singing to the harvest fields, the
earth would blossom like the rose, want
for food would become unknown, and
"the nations would learn war no more."

If Christ should come to reign on

earth, he would overthrow the great trusts and combines that have cornered and placed exorbitant prices upon the necessaries of life. The vast resources of fuel, oil, water, timber, foodstuffs and materials for clothing, would no longer be under the control of a few greedy men, but would be reduced to reasonable prices and placed within reach of the industrious poor and all men would come to live in comfort.

Under the reign of Christ, the white-slave traffic would disappear, the brothel would be unknown and peace and purity would come back to wretched multitudes who have become embruted by the cruel lusts of men; there would be home-comings, reunions, happy hearts and singing in many homes made desolate by sin.

The coming of Jesus to earth would put an end to all sectarianism, and denominational strife. No longer would there be waste of time and resources, building altar against altar. Such an event would mean peace on earth and good will to men. People would forget what churches they had been members of in their fraternal love and harmony. Such an event would change the whole economy of our present state of civilization and society. The very thought of Christ in Jerusalem, would paralyze all the work and ways of Satan and vice and thrill the world with new conception of life and love for holiness. It would mean the casting out of all that is evil and the lifting up of all that is good.

If Christ should come back to Jerusalem and set up his kingdom there, misrule would disappear and political corruption would cease, the conditions that foster and produce poverty, disease, crime, sorrow and sin would vanish away and the knowledge of the glory of the Lord would fill the earth as the waters cover the sea. We can but wish that Jesus Christ would come and say to this stormy human sea, "Peace be still" and hush all the harsh noise and cruel strife and give the tired old world a long, sweet rest. Go search the Scriptures and you will find that they teach Christ will come back to earth again.

CHAPTER V.

FULL REDEMPTION IN CHRIST.

"For this purpose the Son of God was manifested, that he might destroy the works of the devil." 1 John 3:8.

Had there been no sin, there would have been no need for an atonement; the entrance of sin into the world, made the atonement necessary.

In the nature of things, the atonement must meet all the necessities of the case; it must reach as far in its efficacy to restore, as sin has gone to destroy.

The redemptive scheme proposes to restore to man, through the merit of the Second Adam, who never fell, all he lost through the first Adam, who did fall.

We have no sympathy with any

view of the atonement which puts any limit to the virtue of the blood of Christ. We cannot believe that God could conceive of providing a remedy which would not, in every way, be adequate to the disease.

Without doubt, it is the mission of Christ to separate from man, that which separated man from God, in order to his restoration to God. Sin brought that separation and Christ was manifested that he might take away our sins and he can take away our sins, for "He is able to save to the uttermost, all who come unto God by him."

It is high time that the idea of a limited atonement be forever banished from the pulpit and driven out of the church. The whole tenor of the New Testament teaches that Jesus Christ by the grace of God, tasted death for every man, and that the blood of Jesus Christ cleanseth from all sin.

There is an old exploded theory that

Jesus Christ came into the world and died to save men from hell and to save men in heaven, but the Scriptures teach that Jesus Christ came into the world and died to save men from *sin* and to save them in *this world*. The man who is saved from sin need have no fear of hell, and the man who is saved in this world, if faithful, may be sure of heaven in the world to come. It is sin that makes hell a possibility—an awful certainty. The taking away of sin settles the question of the future state. In the nature of things, there can be no hell for a holy man, and in the end, there can be nothing but hell for an unholy man.

One would be quite surprised, if stopping in some great hotel in New York, on hearing a noise in a hall of the building, he should look into the place and find Rockefeller, Morgan and Carnegie mounted on hobby-horses, whip in hand, riding for dear life. Sixty years ago, they no doubt, greatly enjoyed such sport, but they have outgrown that sort of amusement, and sixty years from now, they will get no more amusement out of bank stocks, mortgages, deeds, railroads, oil tanks, refineries, greenbacks and gold, than they get out of hobby-horses now.

This is true of all human beings. The petted woman of wealth, a few years ago, was delighted with dol's, but she could not entertain herself with them now; so it will be with diamonds; a few years hence, they will mean no more to her than bits of sand.

In the nature of things, the spirit must go forward; it cannot stop and be content with things that perish. Spirit cannot feed on matter. "What would it profit a man if he gained the whole world"? All of it would not make one repast for his soul, but the soul would rise from such a feast hungry, disgusted and crying for a crumb of the bread of life, and for water from the wells of salvation. The nature of the soul is such that it must be pure to be happy. Holiness is heaven to the soul.

To find holiness, is for the wandering soul of man to get back home, to rest and rejoice in communion with God, the in- finite source of all holiness. Sin is tor- ture to the soul, and in the nature of things it must be so. Whatever inven- tions men may seek out, whatever di- versions they may delude themselves with, in the end, sin will kindle a fire of torment in the soul. There is com- ing a time, and it is coming more swift- ly than the swallow's wing, when the whole universe will become a quench- less crater of hell to the soul that hates holiness and loves sin.

No doctrine or scheme of salvation which does not provide for a full de- liverance from sin, can satisfy the de- mands of our nature or meet our actual needs. We have already seen that, in the very constitution and nature of the soul, it must be holy, pure from sin, or it must be miserable. Sin is a hot cinder in the eye of the soul. To be happy, the soul must get back to God. But God is holy and cannot look upon sin with allowance; he cannot permit, excuse or apologize for sin. He has made an atonement for sin; Jesus Christ has come to destroy the works of the devil, he can take away our sins and his blood cleanseth from all sin. Outside of him there is no help, but he is abundantly able to save

Let us be done forever with small views of Christ, and little, narrow conceptions of the atonement he has made for the sins of the world. In him there is full and free redemption for all men from a'l sin. He can forgive all transgressions, take away all guilt, impart the new life, cleanse out the old sin life and in every way, fit the once polluted and sinful soul, for the habitation of the Holy Ghost, the companionship of saints and angels.

In contemplating the atonement, the full salvation which Jesus Christ hath

wrought for those who come to him
and trust in him, let it be remembered
that in him dwelleth all the fulness of
the godhead bodily. Jesus Christ did
not begin his conscious existence in
Bethlehem on the night of the Nativity,
when the shouts of the angels startled
the shepherds who watched their flocks
on Judean hills. The conception of an
ordinary man is the beginning of a new
existence, a new intelligent being which
did not exist before, not so with
Christ. He was conceived of the Holy
Ghost. Mary had no part in the gene-
ration of the spirit of Christ; he was
from the eternities. He did not then
begin to exist; he had always existed.

The virgin became the honored instru-
ment for the clothing of his eternal
spirit in human form; through her, God
was manifest in the flesh; she imparted
nothing of her fallen or sinful nature
to his spotless spirit, for his spirit was
complete in all the fulness of absolute
perfection before the conception. She
contributed to giving that spirit a body

in which to live, love and labor, teach, suffer and die. There is no sin in the body, mere matter, hence the absolute sinlessness of Christ. It is the eternal, sinless One, this omnipresent, omnipotent, infinitely compassionate Christ, and he alone, who can lift us out of sin, back into holiness, oneness and communion with God.

www.ingramcontent.com/pod-product-compliance
Lightning Source LLC
Chambersburg PA
CBHW020521030426
42337CB00011B/505